The Nonprofit Starter Kit:  A Simple Guide to Preparing Bylaws and Articles of Incorporation

By:  Eric Nichols

# Acknowledgements

The more books I write, the more I realize the hardest part is the Acknowledgements. There are so many family and friends who are worthy of being acknowledged. However, I'm only human, and like most humans, I cannot possibly remember every single person who has made an impact on my life. With that said, let me thank God for placing so many wonderful people in my life and for blessing me with the special talent to do what I do. God is good all the time and has always been right on time. A big thank you to my entire family and close friends (you know who you are). Thanks for your kindness, well wishes, and moral support. I truly appreciate you all and couldn't ask for a more loving family.

To my beautiful mother, Linda, who is and always will be my Queen. We have a unique bond that has allowed us to weather some of the toughest storms together. And you never cease to amaze me with your strength and determination to survive. Thank you for bringing me into this world and for loving me the way only a mother can (unconditionally). To LaTicia Davis, my editor and friend, who tirelessly worked to polish this project with her amazing insights and creativity, that ultimately has this short powerfully, packed book shining bright like a diamond. Thank you.

A very special thanks to the many men and women who taught me a little something about life and about myself: Rosanda Anderson, Johnathan Webster, Eugene (Geno) Richards, Isaiah Crompton, Irma Carson, Aunt Nett, Art (Uncle Bubba) Powell, Rueben Casey, Marcus Tomlin, Dirk Johnson, Aunt Diane, James E. Burton, Jr., Danny Morrison, Daylan Powell, Monique Nichols, Aunt Sivi, Lloyd Gamble, Kevin Turner, Chris and CeCe Marzette, Floyd Wilkerson, Uncle Al, David Williams, Deondre Brown, Joey and Christy Porter, Brian Hooks, Uncle Glen, Fabious Worthy, Kris Evans, Shawn Glinton, Rod Johnson, Anthony Johnson, Willie Nichols II & III, Shartra Avila, Cynthia Pendleton, Lea Hartdige, Daphne Worthy, Lil Rodney, Peggy Starks, Wesley Davis, Susie Wells, Rufus Hill, Derrick Dickerson, Lovie Dean, A.J. Nichols, Vernon Strong, Shelley Jones, Patrick McKenzie, Ken and Pat Shiloh, Lewis and Rochelle Neil, Aunt Vicky, Milton and Avis Henderson. You have all inspired me in some way. Thank you.

To the mentor I admire most: Steve Harvey. Thanks for leading by example.

To my brothers, Darren and Torrey, and my sister, Shon: Our Daddy did a great job teaching us to stick together and love one another unconditionally. You three are truly blessings sent from above. Thanks for loving me, having my back, believing in me, and for having the courage to "pull my coattail" when necessary. I love y'all.

## Dedications

This book is dedicated to every little kid in America who was born into adversity with dreams to one day become a prosperous and successful person and to the memory of my beloved brother, Derrick DeShawn Nichols, to my Grandparents Curtis E. Nichols, Olivia Nichols, Leola Burton and to my father Curtis E. Nichols, Jr.

The Lord is my light and my salvation;

Whom shall I fear?

The lord is the strength of my life;

Of whom shall I be afraid?

Psalm 27:1

## A Word from the Author

As the founder of a nonprofit organization and an experienced grant writer for more than two decades, I know firsthand that starting a nonprofit organization is difficult and time consuming. Even harder is drafting the Bylaws and Articles of Incorporation. My book, *The Nonprofit Starter Kit: A Simple Guide to Preparing Bylaws and Articles of Incorporation* shows you how to easily construct a professional-looking package and register with the Secretary of State.

This book has been years in the making, as it follows the outlines and methods that I have used successfully in assisting the founders of nonprofit organizations over the years. This book was originally comprised of over 200 pages. Although it was helpful, much of the information was unnecessary. After carefully reading and weighing its full contents, I eliminated what I could, while preserving its most pertinent information to insure you the simplest, safest, and most successful process.

It really works. A few clients have contacted me regarding their success and have let me know how pleased they were to discover for themselves just how easy it is to follow along. Plus, all have reported a great savings in time and money by doing it themselves.

In the beginning, I paid a family member $200 to teach me how to prepare Bylaws. Wanting to know as much about how it works as possible, I then sought additional information regarding Bylaws and nonprofit organizations online and in public libraries. Since drafting my own Bylaws, I have met several people who were interested in starting their own nonprofit agency, motorcycle club, social club or religious corporation. These individuals were all stuck in the same predicament of not knowing the first thing about drafting Bylaws or preparing Articles of Incorporation. All of the people I met who were under the same unfortunate set of circumstances were people who genuinely wanted to help others through their nonprofits. Therefore, I wanted to help them to help others.

So, I wrote this short book as a guide and starter kit for anyone who wants to know how to prepare and draft bylaws. Now, they can do so at a far less price (90% less) than what it cost me.

Read it. Apply It. Share it. Help someone else to help others.

Sincerely,

## TABLE OF CONTENTS

## FREQUENTLY ASKED QUESTONS

**What are bylaws?**

Bylaws are rules adopted by an organization for managing its internal affairs.

**What are Articles of Incorporation?**

Articles of Incorporation are a nonfictional prose composition forming an independent part of a corporation.

**What are Religious Corporations?**

Religious Corporations are corporations organized to operate a church or to be otherwise structured for primarily or exclusively **religious** purposes.

**What are Public Benefit Corporations?**

A corporation organized exclusively for **charitable** purposes within the meaning of Internal Revenue Code, Section 501(c) (3).

**What are Mutual Benefit Corporations?**

A Mutual Benefit Corporation is a corporation organized for other than religious, charitable, civic league or social welfare purposes and planning to obtain tax exempt status under provisions other than State Revenue and Taxation Codes, Internal Revenue Section 501 (c)(4), or not planning to be tax exempt at all.

**Where do I file?**

Documents can be delivered by mail to the Secretary of State in your state of residence. To facilitate the processing of documents mailed to their office, a self-addressed envelope and letter referencing the corporate name, a return address, and the name and telephone number of the person submitting the document should also be submitted. If delivering documents in person (drop off), check with the Secretary of State for the hours of business and office locations.

**Do I need an attorney?**

It is recommended that legal counsel be consulted for advice regarding the proposed corporation's specific business needs, which may require the inclusion of special article provisions.

**How do I draft my own bylaws?**

Drafting your own Bylaws is easy. Just follow the step-by-step instructions comprised of the twenty-nine articles in this book, using the actual Bylaws of a corporation as a guide to draft your own.

## Step 1: (Articles I – VI)

*The preparer of the Bylaws should follow Step 1 by comprising Articles I through VI. These articles consist of the corporation's Name, offices (address), Objectives and Purposes, Nonpartisan Activities, the Construction of Definitions, the Dedication of Assets, and its Membership. These articles should reflect the principles of the corporation.*

*The following is an example of Articles I though VI:*

## BYLAWS

## 4 NEW DIRECTIONS

### A California Nonprofit Public Benefit Corporation

### ARTICLE I

### Name

The name if this corporation is 4 NEW DIRECTIONS

### Article II

### Offices

The principal office for the transaction of activities and affairs of this corporation is located at 1004 W. Derrick Street, Bakersfield CA, 93304, in the County of Kern, State of California. The Board of Directors may change the location of the principal office. Any such change of location must be noted by the Secretary of these Bylaws opposite this Article; alternatively, this Article may be amended to state the new location.

The Board may, at any time, establish branch or subordinate offices at any place or places where this corporation is qualified to conduct its activities.

### Article III

### Objectives and Purposes
### Nonpartisan Activities

This corporation is organized for public benefit, charitable, and educational purposes. In the context of these general purposes, the corporation shall act to: 1) Provide a well-rounded educational support program for youth whose parents are incarcerated or on parole in effort to promote educational success and develop greater social skills; 2) Ensure that the individual's transition from prison to the community is safe and successful; 3) To obtain the relief of wrongly-convicted prisoners; and 4) Carry on other charitable and educational activities associated with these goals, as allowed by law.

Also, in the context of these purposes, the corporation shall not, except to an insubstantial degree, engage in any activities or exercise any powers that do not further the purpose of this corporation, and the corporation shall not carry on any activities not permitted to be carried on by: (a) A corporation exempt from federal income tax under Internal Revenue Code, Section 501 (c)(3) or the corresponding provision of any future United States Internal Revenue law; or (b) A corporation, contributions to which are deductible under Internal Revenue Code, Section 170(c)(2) or the corresponding provision of any future United States Internal Revenue law.

***The context of general purposes may vary in the amount of goals.

## ARTICLE IV

### Construction and Definitions

Unless the context requires otherwise, the general provisions, rules of construction and definitions in California Nonprofit Corporation law shall govern the construction of these Bylaws. Without limiting the generality of the preceding sentence, the masculine gender includes the feminine and neuter, the singular includes the plural, the plural includes the singular, and the term "person' includes both and legal entity and natural person.

## ARTICLE V

### Dedication of Assets

This corporation's assets are irrevocably dedicated to public benefit and charitable purposes, as set forth in Article III.

No part of the net earnings, properties, or assets of the corporation shall inure to the benefit of any of its directors, trustees, officers, private shareholders or members, or to the individuals, provided, however, that this provision shall not prevent the payment to any such person of reasonable compensation for services performed for the corporation if such compensation is otherwise permitted by these Bylaws and is fixed by resolution of the Board; and such person or persons shall not be entitled to share in the distribution of this corporation. On the winding up and dissolution of this corporation, after paying or adequately providing for debts, obligations, and liabilities of the corporation, the remaining assets of this corporation shall be distributed to such organization (or organizations) organized and operated exclusively for charitable purposes which has establish its tax-exempt status under Internal Revenue Code, Section (c)(3) (or corresponding provisions of any future federal internal law).

## ARTICLE VI

### Membership

This corporation shall have no voting members within the meaning of the Nonprofit Corporation Law. Any action which would otherwise require approval by a majority of all members or approval by the members shall require only the approval of the Board of Directors.

The corporation's Board of Directors may, in its discretion, admit individuals to one or more classes of nonvoting members; the class or classes shall have such rights and obligations as the Board finds appropriate.

## Step 2: (Articles VII – XII)

*The preparer of the Bylaws should follow Step 2 by comprising Articles VII – XII that consist of the corporation's Powers and the Duties of the Board of Directors, the Composition of Board of Directors, the Election and Term of Directors, Restriction on Interested Persons as Directors, Meetings of the Board of Directors and Regular and Annual Meetings of the Board of Directors. These items should reflect the specific purpose of the corporation.*

*The following is an example of Articles VII though XII:*

## ARTICLE VII

## Powers and Duties of Board of Directors

Subject to the provisions and limitations of the California Nonprofit Public Benefit Corporation Law and other applicable laws, the activities and affairs of the corporation shall be conducted and all corporate powers exercised by, or under the authority and direction of, the Board of Directors. It shall be the duty of the Directors to:

(a) Perform any and all duties imposed on them, collectively or individually, by law, by the Articles of Incorporation of this corporation, or by these Bylaws;

(b) Appoint and remove, at the pleasure of the Board, all corporate officers, agents, and employees; prescribe powers and duties for them as are consistent with the law, the Articles of Incorporation, and these Bylaws; fix their compensation; and as the Board deems necessary or appropriate, require from them security for faithful service;

(c) Meet at such times and places as required by these Bylaws;

(d) As the Board deems necessary or appropriate, change the principal office or the principal business office in California from one location to another; cause the corporation to be qualified to conduct its activities in any other state, territory, dependency, or country; conduct its activities in or outside California; and designate a place in or outside California for holding any meeting of members;

(e) Register their addresses, telephone numbers, fax numbers, and any electronic mail address that they use with the Secretary of the corporation, and notices of meeting mailed (first-class mail, postage prepaid), telephoned (as reasonably expected to communicate that notice promptly to the director or left on a voice messaging system or other system or technology designed to record and communicate messages to the director), or sent by fax or by electronic mail at such registered addresses or locations shall be valid notices thereof.

The Board of Directors may delegate the management of the activities of the corporation to any person or persons, including an executive committee, however composed, provided that the activities and affairs of the corporation shall be managed and all the corporate powers shall be exercised under the ultimate direction of the Board.

## ARTICLE VIII

### Composition of Board of Directors

The Board of Directors shall consist of at least five, but no more than seven directors, unless changed by amendment to these Bylaws. The exact number of directors shall be fixed, within those limits, by a resolution adopted by the Board of Directors.

## ARTICLE IX

### Election and Term of Directors

The original directors shall serve staggered terms of two or three years, determined by random draw. Thereafter, at the annual meeting of the Board of Directors, new directors for vacant positions shall be elected by a majority vote of the then sitting Board to serve for a term of three years or until their successors are elected and qualify. A director may serve two consecutive terms and unlimited non-consecutive terms, except that serving one year or less of an unexpired term shall not be considered as one of the two consecutive terms.

## ARTICLE X

### Restriction on Interested Persons as Directors

No more than 49 percent of the persons serving on the Board may be "interested persons." An interested person is: (a) Any person compensated by the corporation for services rendered to it within the previous 12 months, whether as a full-time or part-time employee, independent contractor, or otherwise, excluding any reasonable compensation paid to a director as director ; and (b) Any brother, sister, ancestor, descendant, spouse, brother-in-law, sister-in-law, mother-in-law, or father-in-law of such person. However, any violation of this paragraph shall not affect the validity or enforceability of transactions entered into by the corporation.

## ARTICLE XI

### Meetings of the Board of Directors

(a) Meetings of the Board shall be held at any place within or outside California that has been designated by resolution of the Board or in the notice of the meeting or, if not so designated, at the principal office of the corporation.

(b) Any Board meeting may be held by conference telephone, video screen communication, or other communications equipment. Participation in a meeting under this Article shall constitute presence in person at the meeting, if both of the following apply:

1. Each participating member can communicate concurrently with all other members; and
2. Each member is provided the means of participating in all matters before the Board, including the capacity to propose or to interpose an objection to a specific action to be taken by the corporation.

# ARTICLE XII

## Regular and Annual Meetings of the Board of Directors

Regular meeting of the Board of Directors shall be held no less than 4 times per year at a site designated from time to time by resolution of the board. Notice of such regular meetings shall be given as determined by resolution of the Board.

An annual meeting of the Board of Directors shall be held in the month of July for purposes of organization, election of directors, and transaction of other business, unless the Board fixes another date or time. If the schedule falls on a legal holiday, the meeting shall be held on the next full business day. Notice of this annual meeting is not required.

## Step 3: (Articles XIII – XIX)

*The preparer of the Bylaws should follow Step 3 by comprising Articles XIII – XIX that consist of the corporation's Special Meetings of Board of Directors, Quorum and Related Matters, Vacancies on Board of Directors, Compensation of Board of Directors, Committees of Board of Directors, the Meetings and Actions of Committees, and the Officers of the Corporation. These articles should reflect the specific actions of the Board of Directors and its committees.*

*The following is an example of Articles XIII though XIX:*

### ARTICLE XIII

### Special Meetings of Board of Directors

Special meetings of the Board of Directors may be called by any officer or by any 2 directors and such meetings shall be held at the place designated by the person or persons who call the meeting.

Notice of the time and place of special meetings shall be given to each director by: (a) Personal delivery of written notice; (b) First-class mail, postage prepaid; (c) Telephone, including a voice messaging system or other system of technology designed to record and communicate messages, either directly to the director or to the person at the director's office who would be reasonably expected to communicate that notice promptly to the director; (d) Facsimile transmission; (e) Electronic mail; or (f) Other electronic means. All such notices shall be given or sent to the director's address or telephone number as shown on the corporation's records.

Notices sent by first-class mail shall be deposited in the United States mail at least four (4) days prior to the date set for the meeting. Notices given by personal delivery, telephone, facsimile transmission, or electronic mail shall be delivered, telephoned, transmitted, or sent, respectively, at least 72 hours prior to the time set for the meeting.

The notice shall state the time and place of the meeting. The notice does not need to specify the purpose of the meeting.

### ARTICLE XIV

### Quorum and Related Matters

(a)     A quorum for the transaction of any business except adjournment shall consist of a simple majority of the authorized number of directors. A majority of such quorum shall decide any question that may come before the meeting subject to more stringent provision of the Articles of Incorporation or Bylaws of this corporation, or the California Nonprofit Public Benefit Corporation Law, including, without limitation, those provisions relating to (i) approval of contracts or transactions between the corporation and one or more directors or between this corporation and any entity in which a director has a material financial interest, (ii) creation of and appointments to committees of the Board, and (iii) indemnification of directors.

(b)     At a meeting at which quorum is initially present, directors may continue to transact business even after some directors have left, provided that any action taken is approved by at least a majority of the quorum required for the meeting.

(c)     Notice of a meeting need not be given to any director who, either before or after the meeting, signs a waiver of notice, a written consent to the holding of the meeting, or an approval of the minutes of the meeting. The waiver of notice or consent need not specify the purpose of the meeting. All such waivers, consents, and approvals shall be filed with the corporate records or made part of the minutes of the meetings. Notice of a meeting need not be given to any director who attends the meeting and who, before or at the beginning of the meeting, does not protest the lack of notice to her or him.

(d)     A majority of the directors present, whether or not a quorum is present, may adjourn the meeting 24 hours or less without further notice. If the meeting is adjourned for more than 24 hours, notice of the adjournment to another time or place shall be given prior to the time of the adjourned meeting to those directors who were not present at the time of the adjournment.

(e)     Any action the Board is required or permitted to take may be taken without a meeting if all Board members consent in writing to the action; provided, however, that the consent to any director has material financial interest in a transaction to which the corporation is a party and who is an "interested director' as defined in the Corporation's Code, Section 5233, shall not be required for approval of that transaction. Such action by written consent shall have the same force and effect as any other validly approved action of the Board. All such consents shall be filed with the minutes of the proceedings of the Board.

## ARTICLE XV

### Vacancies on Board of Directors

A vacancy or vacancies on the Board of Directors shall occur in the event of: (a) The death, removal, or resignation of any director; (b) The declaration by resolution of the Board of Directors of a vacancy in the office of the director who has been convicted of a felony, declared of unsound mind by court order, or found by order of judgment of any court to have breached a duty under California Nonprofit Public Benefit Corporation Law, Chapter 2, Article 3; or (c) The increase in authorized directors.

(a) Any director may resign effective upon giving written notice to the President or to the Secretary of the Board, unless the notice specifies a later time for the effectiveness of such resignation. If the resignation specifies effectiveness at a future time, a successor may be elected to take office on the date the resignation becomes effective. Notwithstanding the foregoing, except upon notice to the Attorney General of the State of California, no director may resign if such resignation would leave the corporation without a duly elected director or directors in charge of its affairs.

(b) Directors may be removed at any time, with or without cause, by the vote of a majority of the directors currently in office. Any vacancy caused by the removal of a director shall be filled as provided in Paragraph (c) of this article (Article XV). Any director who does not attend three (3) successive meeting of the Board in any one calendar year may be subject to removal by the Board.

(c) Vacancies on the Board may be filled by approval of the Board or, if the number directors then in office is less than a quorum, by (1) the unanimous written consent of the directors then in office, (2) the affirmative vote of a majority of the directors then in office at a meeting held according to notice or waivers of notice complying with Corporations Code, Section 5211, or (3) a sole remaining director.

(d) Any reduction of the authorized number of directors shall not result in any directors being removed before his or her time of office expires.

## ARTICLE XVI

### Compensation and Reimbursement of Directors

Directors and officers shall serve without compensation. Directors may receive such reimbursement of expenses as the Board may establish by resolution to be just and reasonable as to the Corporation at the time that the resolution is adopted.

## ARTICLE XVII

### Committees of Board of Directors

The Board, by resolution adopted by a majority of directors then in office, may create one or more committees, each consisting of two or more directors, to serve at the pleasure of the Board. Appointments to the committees of the Board shall be by majority vote of the directors then in office. The Board may appoint one of more directors as alternate members of any such committee, who may replace any absent member at any meeting. Any such committee shall have all the authority of the Board to the extent provided in the Board resolution, except that no committee, regardless of Board resolution, may:

(a) Take any final action on any matter that, under these Bylaws or under the California Nonprofit Public Benefit Corporation Law, also requires approval of a majority of the Board;

(b) Fill vacancies on the Board on any committee of the Board;

(c) Fix reimbursement of expenses of directors in serving on the Board or on any committee;

(d) Amend or repeal Bylaws or adopt new Bylaws;

(e) Amend or repeal any resolution of the Board by its express terms is not so amendable or repealable;

(f) Create any other committees of the Board or appoint the members of committees of the Board;

(g) Expend corporate funds to support a nominee for director if more people have been nominated for director than can be elected; or

(h) Approve any contract or transaction to which the corporation is a party and in which one or more of its directors has a material financial interest except as special approval is provided for in Corporations Code, Section 5233(d)(3).

## ARTICLE XVIII

### Meetings and Actions of Committees

Meetings and actions of committees of the Board shall be governed by, held, and taken under the provisions of these Bylaws concerning meetings and other Board actions, except that the time for general meetings of such committees may be set either by Board resolution or, if none, by resolution of the committee. Minutes of each meeting shall be kept and shall be filed with the corporate records. The Board may adopt rules for the governance of any committee as long as the rules are consistent with these Bylaws. If the Board has not adopted rules, the committee may do so.

# ARTICLE XIX

## Officers of the Corporation

(a) The officers of this corporation shall be a President, a Secretary, and a Chief Financial Officer. The corporation, at the Board's discretion, may also have one or more Vice Presidents, one or more Assistant Secretaries, one or more Assistant Treasurers, and such other officers as may be appointed under this article (Article XIX) of these Bylaws.

Any number of offices may be held by the same person, except that neither the secretary nor the chief financial officer may serve concurrently as the president of the Board.

(b) The officers of this corporation shall be chosen annually by the Board and shall serve at the pleasure of the Board, subject to the rights of any officer under any employment contract.

(c) The Board may appoint and authorize the President or another officer to appoint other officers that the corporation may require. Each appointed officer shall have the title and authority, hold office for the period, and perform the duties specified in the Bylaws or established by the Board.

(d) Without prejudice to the rights of any officer under an employment contract, the Board may remove any officer with or without cause. An officer who was not chosen by the Board may be removed by any other officer on whom the Board confers the power of removal.

(e) Any officer may resign at any time upon providing written notice to the Board. The resignation shall take effect on the date the notice is received or at any later time specified in the notice. Unless otherwise specified in the notice, the resignation need not be accepted to be effective. Any resignation shall be without prejudice to any rights of the corporation under any contract to which the officer is a party.

(f) A vacancy in any office because of death, resignation, removal, disqualification, or any other cause shall be filled in the manner prescribed in these Bylaws for normal appointment to that office, provided, however, that the vacancies need not be filled on an annual basis.

## Step 4: (Articles XX – XXV)

*The preparer of the Bylaws should follow Step 4 by comprising Articles XX – XXV that consists of the Responsibilities of Officers, Contracts with Directors and Officers, Loans to Directors and Officers, Indemnification, Insurance and Maintenance of Corporate Records. These articles reflect the specific duties assigned to officers of the corporation.*

*The following is an example of Articles XX though XXV:*

## ARTICLE XX

## Responsibilities of Officers

(a) <u>President</u>: Subject to the control of the Board, the President shall be the general manager of the corporation and shall supervise, direct, and control the corporation's activities, affairs, and officers. The President shall preside at all Board meeting.  The President shall have such other powers and duties as the Board or Bylaws may require.

(b) <u>Vice President</u>: If the President is absent or disabled, the Vice President, if any, in order of their rank as fixed by the Board, or if not ranked, a Vice President designated by the Board, shall perform all duties of the President.  When so acting, a Vice President shall have all powers of and be subjected to all restrictions on the President.  The Vice President shall have such other powers and perform such duties as the Board or the Bylaws may require.

(c) <u>Secretary</u>: The Secretary shall keep or cause to be kept, at the corporation's principal office or such other place as the Board may direct, a book of minutes of all meetings, proceedings and actions of the Board and of committees of the Board. The minutes of these meetings shall include the time and place of the meeting, meeting type (annual, general, or special), and the names of persons present. For special meetings, the record should also include how the meeting was authorized and what notice as given.

The Secretary shall keep or cause to be kept, at the principal California office, a copy of the Articles of Incorporation and Bylaws, as amended to date.

The Secretary shall give, or cause to be given, notice of all meetings of the Board and committees of the Board that these Bylaws require to be given.  The Secretary shall keep the corporate seal, if any, in save custody and shall have such other powers and perform other duties as the Board or Bylaws may require.

(d) <u>Chief Financial Officer</u>:  The Chief Financial Officer shall keep and maintain, or cause to be kept and maintained, adequate and correct books and accounts of the corporation's properties and transactions. The Chief Financial Officer shall send or cause to be given to the directors such financial statements and reports that are required to be given by law, by these Bylaws, or by the Board.  The books of account shall be open to inspections by any director at all reasonable times.

The Chief Financial Officer shall (i) deposit, or cause to be deposited, all money and other valuables in the name and to the credit of the corporation with such depositories as the Board designates; (ii) disburse the corporation's funds as the Board may order; (iii) render to the President and the Board, when requested, an account of all transactions as Chief Financial Officer and of the financial condition of the corporation; and (iv) have such other powers and perform such other duties as the Board or Bylaws may require.

If required by the Board, the Chief Financial Officer shall give the corporation a bond in the amount and with the surety or sureties specified by the Board for the faithful performance of the duties of the office and for restoration to the corporation of all of its books, papers, vouchers, money, and other property of every kind in the possession or under control of the Chief Financial Officer on his or her death, resignation, retirement, or removal from office.

## ARTICLE XXI

### Contracts with Directors and Officers

No director of this corporation nor any other corporation, firm, association, or other entity in which one or more of this corporation's directors have a material financial interest, shall be interested directly or indirectly, in any contract or transaction with the corporation unless: (a) The material facts regarding that director's financial interest in such contract or transaction or regarding such common directorship, officership, or financial interest are fully disclosed in good faith and noted in the minutes, or are known to all members of the Board prior to the Board's consideration of such contract or transaction; (b) Such contract or transaction is authorized in good faith by the majority of the Board by a vote sufficient for that purpose without counting the votes of interested directors; (c) before authorizing or approving the transaction, the Board considers and in good faith decides after reasonable investigation, that the corporation could not obtain a more advantageous arrangement with reasonable effort under the circumstances; and (d) The corporation, for its own benefit, enters into the transaction which is fair and reasonable to the corporation at the time the transaction is entered into.

This Article does not apply to a transaction that is part of an educational or charitable program of this corporation if it: (a) Is approved and authorized by the corporation in good faith and without unjustified favoritism; and (b) Results in a benefit to one of more directors or their families because they are in the class of person intended to be benefited by the educational or charitable program of this corporation.

## ARTICLE XXII

### Loans to Directors and Officers

This corporation shall not lend any money or property to, or guarantee the obligation of, any director or officer without the approval of the California Attorney General; provided, however, that the corporation may advance money to a director or officer of the corporation for expenses reasonably anticipated to be incurred in the performance of his or her duties if the director or officer would be entitled to reimbursement for such expenses by the corporation.

## ARTICLE XXIII

### Indemnification

To the fullest extent permitted by the law, this corporation my indemnify its directors, officers, employees, and other persons described in Corporations Code, Section 5238(a), including persons formerly occupying any such positions, against all expense, judgments, fines, settlements, and other amounts actually and reasonably incurred by them in connection with any "proceedings," as that term is used in that sections, and including an action by or in the right of the corporation, by reason of the fact that the person is or was a person described in that section. "Expenses," as used in this bylaw, shall have the same meaning as in that section of the Corporations Code.

On the written request to the Board by any person seeking indemnification under Corporation Code, Section 5238(b) or Section 5238(c), the Board shall promptly decide under Corporations Code, Section 5238(e) whether the applicable standard of conduct set forth in Corporations Code, Sections 5238 (b) and (c) have been met, and if so, the Board shall authorize indemnification.

To the fullest extent permitted by law and except as otherwise determined by the Board in a specific instance, expenses incurred by a person seeking indemnification under Articles XXI or XXII of these Bylaws in defending any proceeding covered by those articles shall be advanced by the corporation before final disposition of the proceeding, on receipt by the corporation of an undertaking by or on behalf of that person that advance will be repaid unless it is ultimately found that the person is entitled to be indemnified by the corporation for those expenses.

## ARTICLE XXIV

### Insurance

This corporation shall have the right, and shall use its best efforts, to purchase and maintain insurance to the full extent permitted by law on behalf of its officers, directors, employees, and other agents, to cover any liability asserted against or incurred by any officer, director, employee, or agent in such capacity of arising from the officer's, director's, or agent's status as such.

## ARTICLE XXV

### Maintenance of Corporate Records

This corporation shall keep:

(a) Adequate and correct books and records of accounts;
(b) Written minutes of the proceedings of its Board and committees of the Board; and
(c) A copy of the corporation's Articles of Incorporation and Bylaws, as amended to current date.

## Step 5: (Articles XXVI – XXIX)

*The preparer of the Bylaws should follow Step 5 (the final step) by comprising Articles XXVI – XXIX that consist of the Director's Rights to Inspect Corporate Records, Required Reports, Amendments to Bylaws, and Prohibition Against Sharing Corporate Assets for Profit. These articles should also reflect the specific purpose of the corporation.*

*The following is an example of Articles XXVI though XXIX:*

## ARTICLE XXVI

### Directors' Right to Inspect Corporate Records

Every director shall have the absolute right at any reasonable time to inspect the corporation's books, records, documents of every kind, physical properties, and the records of each subsidiary. The inspection may be made in person or by the director's agent or attorney. The right of inspection includes the right to copy and make extracts of the documents.

## ARTICLE XXVII

### Required Reports

a) Annual Report

The Board shall cause annual report to be sent to the directors within 120 days after the end of the corporation's fiscal year. That report shall contain the following information:

(1) The assets and liabilities, including any trust funds of the corporation as of the end of the fiscal year;

(2) The principal changes in assets and liabilities, including trust funds;

(3) The corporation's revenue or receipts, both unrestricted and restricted to particular purposes;

(4) Any information required by Paragraph B of this article (Article XXVII) of these Bylaws; and

(5) An independent account's report or, if none, the certificate of an authorized officer of the corporation that such statements were prepared without audit from the corporation's books and records.

The requirement of an annual report shall not apply if the corporation receives less than $25,000 in gross receipts during the fiscal year, provided, however, that the information specified above for inclusion in an annual report must be furnished annually to all directors.

(b) Annual Statement of Certain Transactions and Indemnifications

As part of the annual report to all directors, or as a separate document if no annual report is issued, the corporation shall, within 120 days after the end of the corporation's fiscal year, annually prepare and furnish to each director a statement of any transaction or indemnification of the following kind:

(1) Any transaction: (A) in which the corporation, or its parent or subsidiary, was a party; (B) in which an "interested person" had a direct or indirect material financial interest; and (C) which involved more than $50,000. For this purpose, an "interested person" is:

    i.    Any director or officer of the corporation, or its parent or subsidiary (but mere common directorship shall not be considered an interest); or

    ii.    Any holder of more than 10 percent of the voting power of the corporation, its parent, or its subsidiary.

The statement shall include a brief description of the transaction, the names of interested persons involved, their relationship to the corporation, the nature of their interest in the transaction and, if applicable, the amount of that interest. If the transaction was with a partnership, it should also be stated.

(2) Any indemnifications or advances aggregating more than $10,000 paid during the fiscal year to any officer or director of the corporation under Article XXIII of these Bylaws.

## ARTICLE XXVIII

### Amendments to Bylaws

These Bylaws may be adopted, amended, or repealed by a majority vote of the directors present and voting at a duly held meeting in which a quorum is present, provided that the proposed amendment, repeal, or adoption has been included in the notice of the meeting at which such action to amend, repeal, or adopt is proposed to be taken.

## ARTICLE XXIX

### Prohibition Against Sharing Corporate Assets or Profits

No director, officer, employee, or other person connected with this corporation, or any private individual shall receive at any time any of the net earnings of the pecuniary profit from the operations of the corporation, provided, however, that this provision shall not prevent the payment to any such person of reasonable compensation for services performed for the corporation in effecting any of its public or charitable purposes, provided that such compensation is otherwise permitted by these Bylaws and is fixed by resolution of the Board and such person or persons shall not be entitled to share in the distribution of, and shall not receive, any of the corporate assets on dissolution of the corporation.

On such dissolution or winding up the affairs of the corporation whether voluntary or involuntary, the assets of the corporation then remaining in the hands of the Board, after all debts have been satisfied, shall be distributed as required by the Articles of Corporation of this corporation and not otherwise.

## CERTIFICATE OF SECRETARY

I certify that I am the duly elected and acting Secretary of 4 New Directions, a California nonprofit public benefit corporation; that these Bylaws consisting of twenty-five (21) pages are the Bylaws of this corporation as adopted by the Board of Directors on _____, 2017; and that these Bylaws have not been amended or modified since that date.

Executed on _____, 2017 in Bakersfield, California.

_____, Secretary

## Organizations of California Nonprofit, Nonstock Corporations

In California, nonprofit, nonstock corporations organized for religious, charitable, social, educational, recreational, or similar purposes are formed pursuant to the Nonprofit Corporation Law, commencing with California Corporations Code, Section 5000. The three primary types of nonprofit corporations are namely religious, public benefit and mutual benefit.

The samples within this book have been drafted to meet the minimum statutory requirements. The samples may be used as a guide in preparing the necessary documents to be filed with the Secretary of State. You must first determine the type of nonprofit corporation to be formed and follow the applicable sample. It is strongly recommended that legal counsel be consulted for advice regarding the proposed corporation's specific business needs, which may require the inclusion of special article provisions. The Secretary of State does not provide a standardized form, due to the many possible drafting variations.

In California, Articles of Incorporation must be drafted to include the provisions required by the California Corporations Code. Articles of Incorporation may include other provisions as permitted under California law (such as the name and address of each initial director).

The document should be typed with letters in dark contrast to the paper. Documents that are not suitable for reproductions will be returned unfiled. So make sure everything that you submit is clear and legible.

The file date of Articles of Incorporation is generally the date the document complying with applicable law is received in the Secretary of State's office.

**Article I**: The article must include the name of the corporation.

*The name must be exactly as you want it to appear on the records of the California Secretary of State (or the state in which you are filing).

*Name restrictions apply to most business entities. Please refer to the Name Availability webpage in your state for the business entity name regulations and most common statutory requirements and restrictions relating to the adoption of a business entity name in your state.

**Article II (a)**: One of the following three (3) types of corporations must be listed:

**Mutual Benefit Corporation**: This exact statement is required by California Corporations Code and should not be altered. (Other states may have similar requirements).

**Public Benefit Corporation**: This exact statement is required by California Corporations Code and should not be altered except to include the applicable purpose description. (Other states may have similar requirements).

**Religious Corporation**: This exact statement is required by California Corporations Code and should not be altered. (Other states may have similar requirements).

**Article II(b)**: The statement describing the specific purpose may be included and, in fact, must be included if the corporation is actually organized for public purposes or if the corporation intends to apply for state franchise tax exemption.

**Article III**: The article must include the name of the initial agent for service of process. (This is the most essential requirement of all).

An "agent for service of process' is an individual (director, officer, or any other person, whether or not they are affiliated with the corporation) who resides in California or another corporation designated to accept service of process if the corporation is sued. The agent must also agree to accept service of process on behalf of the corporation prior to designation.

*If an individual is designated as agent, you must include the agent's business or residential street address in California or the state in which you are filing (a P.O. Box address is not acceptable).

*Do not use "in care of," c/o, or abbreviate the name of the city.

*If another corporation is designated as agent, do not include the address of the designated corporation.

*Before another corporation may be designated as agent, that corporation must have previously filed with the Secretary of State a certificate pursuant to the California Corporations Code, Section 1505.

Note: A corporation cannot act as its own agent and no domestic or foreign corporation may file pursuant to Section 1505 unless the corporation is currently authorized to engage in business in California and is in good standing on the records of the California Secretary of State. (Requirements may vary from state to state).

**Articles IV and V** (where applicable): The Franchise Tax Board requires this language before state exemption may be granted.

**Execution**: The articles must be signed by each incorporator, or by each initial director names in the articles. I the initial directors **are** named, each director must both sign and acknowledge the articles.

If the initial directors **are not** named in the articles, the individual(s) executing the document is the incorporator(s) of the corporation.

The name of each incorporator or initial director must be typed beneath their signatures.

*Source: Secretary of State, Business Programs Division, State of California

Some regional offices are only equipped to process the documents that are received in person, over-the-counter. In the State of California, documents submitted by mail must be sent directly to their Sacramento Office at the following address:

Secretary of State
Business Programs Division
1500 11th Street, Third Floor
Sacrament, CA 95814
Attention: Document Filing Support Unit

Documents received by mail in most offices are usually processed based on the date received by their office. Please refer to the Business Entities Mail Processing Times webpage of your state for current mail processing times.

In California, the regional offices are happy to provide over-the-counter services for the following: requests for name reservations; filing of Articles of Incorporation (to form California Corporations); and filing Statement of Designation by Foreign Corporation forms (to qualify out-of-state or out-of-country corporations to transact business in California). Please note: In the State of California, Articles of Incorporation containing a statement of conversion must be filed in their Sacramento office.

(Mutual Benefit Sample*)

Articles of Incorporation

I

The name of this corporation is (Name of Corporation)

II

(a) This corporation is a nonprofit Mutual Benefit Corporation organized under the Nonprofit Mutual Bene
Corporation Law.  The purpose of this corporation is to engage in any lawful act or activity other than
credit union business, for which a corporation may be organized under such law.

(b) The specific purpose of this corporation is to _____

III

The name and address in the State of California of this corporation's initial agent for service of process is:

Name: _____

Address: _____

City: _____ State: _____ Zip Code: _____

IV

Notwithstanding any of the above statements of purposes and powers, this corporation shall not, except to an
insubstantial degree, engage in any activities or exercise any powers that are not in furtherance of the specific
purposes of this corporation.

_____(Signature of the Incorporator)_____
(Name of Incorporator), Incorporator

*This sample should only be used as a guideline in the presentation of the original document for filing with the
Secretary of State.

To form a nonprofit, mutual benefit corporation in California, you can fill out the state's ARTS-MU form or prepare your own document, and submit for filing along with:

- A $30 filing fee.
- A separate non-refundable $15 service fee must also be included, if you drop off the completed form or document.

**Important!** Nonprofit corporations in California are not automatically exempt from paying California franchise tax or income tax each year. For more information about tax requirements and/or applying for tax exempt status in your state, please contact the state's Franchise Tax Board.

- If you need more space of the state-issued form, attach extra pages that are 1-sided and on standard letter-sized paper (8 ½" x 11"). All attachments are made part of the Articles of Incorporation.

Note: Before submitting any form, you should consult with a private attorney for advice about your specific business needs.

(Public Benefit Sample*)

Articles of Incorporation

I

The name of this corporation is <u>(Name of Corporation)</u>

II

(a)  This corporation is a nonprofit Public Benefit Corporation and is not organized for the private gain of any person. It is organized under the Nonprofit Public Benefit Corporation Law for:

        ( ) public purposes.
or  ( ) charitable purposes.
or  ( ) public and charitable purposes.

(b)  The specific purpose of this corporation is to _____

III

The name and address in the State of California of this corporation's initial agent for service of process is:

Name: _____
Address: _____
City: _____ State: _____ Zip Code: _____

IV

(a)  This corporation is organized and operated exclusively for charitable purposes within the meaning of Internal Revenue Code, Section 501(c)(3).

(b)  No substantial part of the activities of this corporation shall consist of carrying on propaganda, or otherwise attempting to influence legislation, and the corporation shall not participate or intervene in any political campaign (including the publishing or distribution of statements) on behalf of any candidate for public office.

V

The property of this corporation is irrevocably dedicated to charitable purposes and no part of the net income or assets of this corporation shall ever inure to the benefit of any director, officer, or member thereof or to the benefit of any private person.  Upon the dissolution or winding up of the corporation, its assets remaining after payment, or provision for payment, of all debts and liabilities of this corporation shall be distributed to a nonprofit fund, foundation or corporation which is organized and operated exclusively for charitable purposes and which has established its tax exempt status under Internal Revenue Code, Section 501(c)(3).

_____(Signature of the Incorporator)_____
(Name of Incorporator), Incorporator

*This sample should only be used as a guideline in the presentation of the original document for filing with the Secretary of State.

To form a nonprofit, public benefit corporation in California, you can fill out the state's ARTS-PU form or prepare your own document, and submit for filing along with:

A $30 filing fee.

A separate non-refundable $15 service fee must also be included, if you drop off the completed form or document.

Important! Nonprofit corporations in California are not automatically exempt from paying California franchise tax or income tax each year. For more information about tax requirements and/or applying for tax exempt status in your state, please contact the state's Franchise Tax Board.

If you need more space of the state-issued form, attach extra pages that are 1-sided and on standard letter-sized paper (8 ½" x 11"). All attachments are made part of the Articles of Incorporation.

Note: Before submitting any form, you should consult with a private attorney for advice about your specific business needs.

(Religious Sample*)

Articles of Incorporation

I

The name of this corporation is (Name of Corporation)

II

(a) This corporation is a Religious Corporation and is not organized for the private gain of any person. It is organized under the Nonprofit Religious Corporation Law for religious purposes.

(b) The specific purpose of this corporation is to _____

III

The name and address in the State of California of this corporation's initial agent for service of process is:

Name: _____

Address: _____

City: _____ State: _____ Zip Code: _____

IV

(a) This corporation is organized and operated exclusively for religious purposes within the meaning of Internal Revenue Code, Section 501(c)(3).

(b) No substantial part of the activities of this corporation shall consist of carrying on propaganda, or otherwise attempting to influence legislation, and the corporation shall not participate or intervene in any political campaign (including the publishing or distribution of statements) on behalf of any candidate for public office.

V

The property of this corporation is irrevocably dedicated to religious purposes and no part of the net income or assets of this corporation shall ever inure to the benefit of any director, officer, or member thereof or to the benefit of any private person. Upon the dissolution or winding up of the corporation, its assets remaining after payment, or provision for payment, of all debts and liabilities of this corporation shall be distributed to a nonprofit fund, foundation or corporation which is organized and operated exclusively for charitable purposes and which has established its tax exempt status under Internal Revenue Code, Section 501(c)(3).

_____(Signature of the Incorporator)_____

(Name of Incorporator), Incorporator

*This sample should only be used as a guideline in the presentation of the original document for filing with the Secretary of State.

To form a nonprofit, religious corporation in California, you can fill out the state's ARTS-RE form or prepare your own document, and submit for filing along with:

- A $30 filing fee.

- A separate non-refundable $15 service fee must also be included, if you drop off the completed form or document.

Important! Nonprofit corporations in California are not automatically exempt from paying California franchise tax or income tax each year. For more information about tax requirements and/or applying for tax exempt status in your state, please contact the state's Franchise Tax Board.

- If you need more space of the state-issued form, attach extra pages that are 1-sided and on standard letter-sized paper (8 ½" x 11").  All attachments are made part of the Articles of Incorporation.

Note:  Before submitting any form, you should consult with a private attorney for advice about your specific business needs.

## Businesses and Corporations

Listed below are major corporations who have adopted Bylaws:

| | | |
|---|---|---|
| Adidas Group | Advance Publications, Inc. | Aetna, Inc. (AET) |
| Aflac, Inc. (AFL) | Alaska Air Group, Inc. (ALK) | Alcatel – Lucent |
| Alcoa Inc. | Alibaba Group. | Allstate Group |
| Altria Group, Inc. | Amazon.com, Inc. | American Airlines Group, Inc. |
| American Electric Power Co., Inc. | American Express Co. | American Greetings Corp. |
| American Intl. Group, Inc. | AmerisourceBergen | Anheuser-Busch InBev |
| Anthem, Inc. | Apple, Inc. | ARAMARK Corp. |
| AT&T Inc. | AutoNation, Inc. | Avon Products, Inc. |
| Bank of America Corp. | Barnes & Noble, Inc. | Baxter International, Inc. |
| Beam Suntroy | Berkshire Hathaway, Inc. | Betrelsmann AG |
| Best Buy Co., Inc. | Blackstone Group LP, The | Blockbuster LLC |
| Boeing Co. | Brink's Co., The | Bristole-Meyers Squibb Co. |
| Brown Shoe Co., Inc. | Brunswich Corp. | Burger King |
| Caleres | Cablevision Systems Corp. | Ceasar's Entertainment corp. |
| Campbell Soup Co. | Catermillar, Inc. | CBS Corp. |
| Century-Link, Inc. | Chevron, Corp. | Chiquita Brands Intl., Inc. |
| Church & Dwight Co., Inc. | Cigna Corp. | Circuit City Stores, Inc. |
| Cisco Systems, Inc. | Citigroup, Inc. | Clorox Co. |
| Coca-Cola Co. | Colgate-Palmolive Co. | Comcast Corp. |
| Continental Airlines, Inc. | Corning, Inc. | Costco Wholesale Corp. |
| Crane Co. | Crown Holding, Inc. | CVS Health |
| Dana Holding Corp. | Darden Restaurants, Inc. | Dean Foods Co. |
| Deere & Co. | Dell, Inc. | Delta Airlines, Inc. |
| Diebold, Inc. | Dish Network Corp. | Walt Disney Co., The |
| Dole Foods Co., Inc. | Dollar Tree | Dr. Peper Snapple Group, Inc. |
| Duke Energy Corp. | Dupont | Easton Corp. |
| Ebay, Inc. | Electronic Arts Inc. | Electronic Data Systems |

## Associations and Organizations

Listed below are organizations who have adopted Bylaws:

| Academic and Educational | Children and Social Services | Religious |
|---|---|---|
| Alpha Delta Kapa | Big Brothers and Sisters of America | African Methodist Episcopal Church |
| Beta Gama Sigma, Inc. | Boy Scouts of America | American Baptist Churches, USA |
| Beta Sigma Phi Intl. | Boys and Girls Club of America | Church of Christ |
| College Board | Camp Fire | Community Church of Christ |
| Education, American Council on | Children's Aid Society | Church of God |
| Educators for World Peace, Intl. Assn of | Feeding America | Church of Jesus Christ |
| English-Speaking Union of the US | 4-H Council, Natl. | Bible Society, American |
| Entomological Society of America | Future Business Leaders of America | Community Churches, Intl. |
| Family Relations, Natl. Council on | Girl Scouts of the USA | Converge Worldwide |
| Freedom of Information Coalition, Natl. | Junior Achievement, USA | Episcopal Church |
| French Institute/Alliance Franchise | | First Church of Christ |
| Genealogical Society, Natl. | **Fraternal** | Free Methodist Church |
| Genetic Assn., American | Elks of the USA | Freedom From Religion Foundation |
| Geological Society of America | Kiwanis Intl. | Gideons Intl. |
| Hemispheric Affairs, Council on | Knights of Columbus | Interfaith Alliance |
| Intl. Education, Institute of | Moose Intl., Inc. | Jehovah's Witnesses |
| Intl. Educational Exchange, Council on | Rotary Intl. | Jewish Congress, American |
| Intl. Law, American Society of | Shriner's Intl. | Mennonite Church USA |
| Irish American Cultural Inst. | | Moravian Church in North America |
| | | Orthodox union |
| | | Pentecostal Assemblies of the World |
| | | United Church of Christ |

Made in the USA
Monee, IL
01 August 2021